COBRAS

BY: ERIC ETHAN

South Bend, Indiana 46617

Gareth Stevens Publishing
MILWAUKEE

For a free color catalog describing Gareth Stevens' list of high-quality books, call 1-800-542-2595 (USA) or 1-800-461-9120 (Canada). Gareth Stevens' Fax: 1-414-225-0377.

Library of Congress Cataloging-in-Publication Data

Ethan, Eric.
        Cobras / by Eric Ethan.
            p. cm. — (Fangs! an imagination library series)
        Includes index.
        Summary: Describes what cobras look like, what they eat, where
they can be found, how they defend themselves, the dangers from
their bites, and the outlook for their future.
        ISBN 0-8368-1428-2
        1. Cobras—Juvenile literature. [1. Cobras. 2. Poisonous
snakes. 3. Snakes.] I. Title. II. Series: Ethan, Eric.
Fangs! an imagination library series.
QL666.064E845   1995
597.96—dc20   95-19260

Published in 1995 by:
Gareth Stevens Publishing
1555 N RiverCenter Drive, Suite 201
Milwaukee WI 53212 USA

Original Text: Eric Ethan
Series Design: Shari Tikus
Cover Design: Karen Knutson
Photo Credits: All photos © Joe McDonald except Pages 7 and 11 © Brian Kenney

Printed in the United States of America
1 2 3 4 5 6 7 8 9 99 98 97 96 95

TABLE OF CONTENTS

What Are Cobras? 4

What Do They Look Like? 6

Where Are They Found? 8

Senses and Hunting 10

What Do They Eat? 14

Self-Defense 16

Cobra Bites 18

Unusual Facts 20

The Future 22

Glossary. 23

Index and Places to
Write for More Information 24

WHAT ARE COBRAS?

Cobras are poisonous snakes found in Africa and Asia. There are six species of cobras. Five species live in Africa. But it is the king cobra, also called the Hamadryad, that people think of first. The king cobra is found in India and the Philippines.

Cobras are sometimes used in street shows in India. These snakes often have their fangs removed or their mouths sewn shut so they cannot hurt their handler.

An Indian cobra, Naja Naja, in a street show.

WHAT DO THEY LOOK LIKE?

Cobras have short wide heads and thin bodies. Most grow to 5-8 feet (1.5-2.5 meters) in length. The king cobra is much larger. They can grow to 16-18 feet (5-5.5 meters) long. Their bodies are covered by flat, tough plates called scales. Cobras must shed their skin to grow. First the old skin becomes dry and thin. Then a new skin forms, and the cobra crawls out of its old one.

If danger is near cobras raise up and flatten their necks. This looks like a hood. It is a warning from the cobra that they may strike.

Most cobras have two spots on the back of their necks. These spots look like eyes.

This Indian cobra is standing up with its neck flattened.

WHERE ARE THEY FOUND?

Most cobras are found in Africa. In the north cobras live in deserts. They make holes in the ground called dens. The central part of Africa is wetter. There cobras live in or near water or up in trees. Southern Africa is like much of India. In both places cobras live in open grassy areas.

King cobras are the only snake known to make nests. They use leaves and twigs like birds do.

It is warm year round in most places where cobras live. Because of this cobras do not **hibernate**.

King cobras, like this one, are the largest poisonous snakes in the world.

SENSES AND HUNTING

Cobras are **predators**. This means they must eat other animals to stay alive. Snakes cannot hear well or see very far. But their tongues are very useful when hunting.

Each time the tongue flicks out of a snakes mouth it tests the air and ground around it. In the snakes mouth is the **Jacobson's organ**. It **analyzes** what the tongue picks up. This helps the cobra track its prey.

*The spots on the back of the
cobra's hood look like eyes.*

Many snakes ambush their prey. This means they stay in one place for a long time until an animal is close enough to strike.

Cobras are hunters. They go after their prey. Cobras do most of their hunting during the day. They do not have special organs to help them see at night like rattlesnakes do.

Cobras may still be able to see better than other snakes. Most snakes have eyes like cats, but cobra eyes have round pupils like a human's.

An Egyptian Banded Cobra.

WHAT DO THEY EAT?

In Africa cobras that hunt on the ground eat rats and mice and other small **mammals**. Water cobras catch frogs and fish. Tree cobras often hunt for birds.

The king cobra of India will also eat rats and mice. But its favorite food is other snakes. It is one of the few snakes known to hunt other snakes for food.

A spectacled Indian cobra.

SELF-DEFENSE

Cobras are shy snakes. If they can they will move away from danger. When they cannot, they stand up and spread their hoods. Cobras can stand up to half their length. This makes them look bigger and more dangerous. Cobras use this to scare other animals away.

This works so well that nonpoisonous snakes copy what cobras do. These snakes have learned that other animals will move away if they stand up and flatten their necks.

Black-necked spitting cobras squirt venom into the eyes of attackers and prey.

COBRA BITES

   Cobra fangs are fixed. They do not fold back when the mouth is closed like other snakes. Because of this cobra fangs are short, less than 1/2 inch (1.3 cm) long.

   Cobras do not let go after they bite. They chew on their victim and inject as much **venom** as they can. When cobras are hunting they inject enough **venom** to kill. But cobras can bite without injecting any venom if they are trying to scare another animal away.

   In Africa spitting cobras squirt venom through their fangs. They aim at the eyes of their prey. This blinds the animals so the cobra can get close enough to bite it.

Cobras have small fangs. They can be hard to see even when the snake is ready to strike.

UNUSUAL FACTS

African spitting cobras can squirt venom 5-6 feet (1.5-1.8 meters). Their venom is very strong and will blind a person if it is not washed out right away.

In India, cobras are used in street shows. Snake charmers play flutes and the cobras look like they move to the music. But cobras cannot hear well. Instead the cobra is watching the flute as it moves back and forth.

When king cobras are angry they can growl like a small dog. The king cobra is believed to be the largest poisonous snake. The largest king cobra on record measured nearly 18 feet (5.5 meters) . A king cobra can inject enough venom to kill a fully grown elephant.

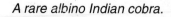

A rare albino Indian cobra.

THE FUTURE

Many cobras live far away from people in deserts and jungle areas. Cobras will be able to live there for a long time to come.

In parts of Africa where people raise cattle or farm they see cobras as dangerous. They kill cobras even though they hunt pests like rats and mice.

In India, people believe it is wrong to kill cobras even though they are poisonous. They know that cobras do not attack people who do not bother them.

GLOSSARY

analyze (AN a lize) - To separate something into its parts to study them.

hibernate (HI ber nate) - To spend the winter in a deep sleep.

Jacobson's organ (JAY kob sons OR gan) - A special pouch in a snake's mouth that analyzes what the tongue picks up.

mammal (MAM el) - A warm blooded animal that has a back bone.

predator (PRED a tor) - An animal that lives by killing and eating other animals.

venom (VE nom) - The poison of snakes.

INDEX

Africa 4, 18, 14, 18, 22
ambush 12
defense 16
dens 8
fangs 4, 18
food 14
hibernate 8
hearing 10, 20
hood 6, 16
hunt 10, 12, 14, 18, 22
India 8, 14, 20, 22
Jacobson's organ 10

King Cobra 4, 6, 8, 14, 20
length 6, 16
predator 10
prey 10, 12
scales 6
Spitting Cobras 18, 20
snake charmers 20
species 4
strike 6, 12
tongue 10
venom 18, 20

PLACES TO WRITE FOR MORE INFORMATION

American Society of Ichthyologists and Herpetologists
US National Museum
Washington, DC 20560

Copeia
American Society of Herpetologists
34th Street and Girard Avenue
Philadelphia, PA 19104

Herpetologists League
1041 New Hampshire Street
Lawrence, KS 66044

Herpetological
1041 New Hampshire Street
Lawrence, KS 66044